Published by:
City of Newcastle Upon Tyne
Newcastle Libraries
Tyne Bridge Publishing, 2020
Modern Photography © Tom Yellowley and Derek Tree
unless otherwise indicated
Layout design: Derek Tree

Cover Artwork © tilartt

Acknowledgements:

The author gratefully acknowledges the major contribution made by the late Newcastle shipping historian and author Dick Keys to the chapters entitled Icebreakers for Russia, Chinese Sailors and Battling Engineers. An enthusiastic and expert researcher, Dick Keys was co-author with Ken Smith of several books, including Down Elswick Slipways, From Walker to the World and Armstrong's River Empire.

Many thanks are also extended to photographer Dr Tom Yellowley for his extensive picture research and for generously contributing his photographs, and to Bill Bell, of the North of England Institute of Mining and Mechanical Engineers, for his kind help, advice and information concerning miners' safety lamps. In addition, grateful acknowledgement is made to Vanessa Histon and Stephen Smith for their proof reading work and last, but by no means least, to Derek Tree, manager, Tyne Bridge Publishing.

The publishers extend their grateful thanks to Ward Philipson Photo Memories for permission to use photos of the 1929 North East Coast Exhibition.
www.photomemoriesarchive.org.uk

CONTENTS

The Castle Keep today.

The story of Newcastle begins with a bridge the Romans constructed across the River Tyne and a fort they built to guard the crossing. The bridge was known as Pons Aelius (the Roman Emperor Hadrian's family name was Aelius) and the fort took its name from the bridge.

Newcastle is named after the New Castle, founded in 1080 on the site of the Roman fort by Robert Curthose, eldest son of William the Conqueror.

Robert ordered the building of the castle after returning from a military foray into Scotland. This early fortress was not built of stone. The stronghold would probably have been a typical early Norman castle featuring ditches and surrounded by a wooden palisade. There might also have been an earth mound (motte) inside the enclosure with a wooden Keep at its top.

Only 15 years after the New Castle was built it saw military action. In 1095, Robert de Mowbray, Earl of Northumbria, rebelled against King William Rufus and took over the fortress. The king came northwards and recaptured the castle after a siege.

Robert Curthose's earth and timber castle was replaced with a stone one during the reign of Henry II. This much stronger fortress was built between 1168 and 1178. Its architect was a man known to history as 'Maurice the Engineer'. Henry II must have been pleased with his work, for Maurice would later be responsible for the construction of Dover Castle.

The second 'New Castle' was built of sandstone and featured a strong, approximately square-shaped Keep. The Castle Keep – constructed between 1172 and 1177 - is today the oldest major building in the city. Its walls are up to 18ft thick and its roof is 81ft from ground level.

Four turrets, the highest a double-turret to carry the flagpole, crown the roof of the Keep. However, these turrets and battlements are not originals and were added in the early 19th century.

Part of the castle's curtain wall survives to the south of the Keep, overlooking the Tyne. Some of this is behind the Bridge Hotel. A postern gate in this south wall leads to the Castle Stairs, which descend to The Close and the Quayside.

The remnants of a tower are also visible, at the rear of the Bridge Hotel, close to the High Level Bridge. Other remains of the castle include those visible on its north eastern side, close to the Dog Leap Stairs.

The original main entrance to the castle was the Baillie or Bailiff Gate, on the south western side of the bailey (courtyard) and very close to the Keep. This entrance, also known as the Great Gate, has vanished.

A number of other buildings were erected in the bailey, including the Great Hall, stables and kitchen. The Great Hall, now demolished, was next to the eastern curtain wall and is believed to have been built during the reign of John (1199-1216). It occupied the site of the present day Vermont Hotel and part of the Moot Hall courtyard.

Accommodation for visiting monarchs was next to the Great Hall. This was probably because the Keep lacked the comforts demanded by royalty. King John, who spent much time in Newcastle, may have lodged in these royal apartments. Yet not all kings stayed in the castle as guests. Scotland's William the Lion and David II were briefly held prisoner there.

Between 1247 and 1250, during the reign of Henry III, the Black Gate was built on the western side of the bailey to provide additional protection for the North Gate. A drawbridge and ditch formed part of the defences. The two upper storeys of the Black Gate were added in the early 17th Century. Further alterations, including a new roof, were made by the Society of Antiquaries of Newcastle upon Tyne in the 1880s.

In 1292, the newly-crowned King of Scotland, John Baliol, came to the castle's Great Hall to do homage to Edward I of England. Edward was consolidating his claim to Scotland and his control of the man he had chosen to occupy the Scottish throne.

The walls of the castle were not to be the only

A view from the top of the Keep

defensive walls built in Newcastle. The Town Walls were constructed in the 13th and 14th centuries to defend Newcastle against invading Scottish armies or other military threats.

In 1265, during the reign of Henry III, a wall tax, known as 'murage', was imposed on townsmen to pay for constructing this barrier, although it is thought that work on building the walls did not start until a few years later in 1272, during the reign of Edward I.

The work was largely paid for by local taxation, although some of the towers and gates were financed by the town's monasteries, wealthy merchants and nobles who owned property in the town.

The Castle Keep and surroundings in the late 18th/early 19th Century.

One story claims that a wealthy townsman was taken prisoner by the Scots during the reign of Edward I and "being at last ransomed by a large sum, he, first of all, began to surround the town with walls". There is no proof this story is true, but perhaps this particular townsman boosted the money already collected through tax and enabled the work to be started.

The Town Walls took many years to build, but were largely complete by the middle of the 14th Century. The Quayside section is believed to have been finished a little later.

Antiquarian John Leland, writing of Newcastle in the 16th century, declared: "The strength and magnificence of the walling of this town far passeth all the walls of the cities of England, and most of the towns of Europe."

The walls, a little over two miles long and built from locally quarried sandstone, featured a walkway along the top, fortified gates, 17 towers and a series of turrets. The dimensions of this impressive barrier varied, generally ranging from 20ft to 30ft high and from 7ft to 10ft thick. There were statues of armed warriors or knights positioned on turret tops.

The Building of the New Castle, 1080, by William Bell Scott. This fine painting gives the impression that the stone castle was constructed in 1080. However, at that date it would have been a wooden structure and was not rebuilt in stone until nearly a century later. The painting is on display at Newcastle Literary & Philosophical Society Library.

To stand any chance of repulsing an attack, good organisation was clearly needed. Accordingly, Newcastle was divided into 24 wards (districts) and the residents of each ward were responsible for the defence of a particular gate or tower.

In 1297, Scots warrior William Wallace led a raid deep into Northumberland following his victory at Stirling Bridge, but he avoided attacking Newcastle after townsmen met him with a show of force. He and his men retreated northwards.

In 1299, after the Scottish defeat at the Battle of Falkirk the previous year, Wallace led another incursion across the border. According to early 19th century historian Eneas Mackenzie (1827), despite the hammer blow of Falkirk, Wallace "still maintained the contest for liberty" and "led his chosen band to the walls of Newcastle, which he assailed in vain, being always repulsed by the valour of the inhabitants". This implies that some sections of the walls were complete by 1299.

An interior view of the Castle Keep. The Keep dates to the 12th Century.

Newcastle was besieged by the Scots twice during the 14th century, but both attacks were unsuccessful. In 1342, David II and his army crossed the border but were repulsed when they tried to capture the town.

A party of 200 defenders sallied forth from a gate by night, surprising soldiers of the besieging Scottish army and taking the Earl of Murray prisoner in his tent. Afterwards the Scots attacked the walls but came up against a strong defence led by the captain of the castle, Sir John Neville.

The second attack came in 1388 when the Second Earl of Douglas and another Scottish force invaded England, raiding as far south as Durham. Afterwards they turned northwards and appeared before the walls of Newcastle.

The Earl of Northumberland had sent his sons, Sir Henry and Sir Ralph Percy and their army to Newcastle to reinforce the garrison and repulse the Scots.

Horse-drawn cabs outside the Black Gate c1890, with the Castle Keep in the background.

Skirmishes developed between the town garrison and the Scottish force immediately outside the walls. During one of these encounters Sir Henry, better known to history as Harry Hotspur, was knocked from his horse by the Earl of Douglas, who captured his opponent's pennon (narrow-shaped standard).

Douglas is said to have challenged Hotspur to take up the fight again if he wished to recover his pennon and the Scots withdrew northwards to Otterburn. Hotspur was determined to recover the pennon rather than have the Scots take it out of Northumberland into their own country. Accordingly, a day or two later he and Sir Ralph, accompanied by their men, left Newcastle in pursuit of Douglas.

However, at Otterburn the Scots won the moonlight battle of Chevy Chase (Cheviot Forest) and Hotspur was taken prisoner. Yet the Scots suffered a serious loss when Douglas was killed. So it seems the survivors of this battle left the scene with decidedly mixed feelings.

A statue of Harry Hotspur at Alnwick by Northumberland sculptor Keith Maddison.

How the interior of the Castle Keep looks today.

THE OLD TYNE BRIDGE

For more than 500 years only one bridge spanned the River Tyne between Newcastle and Gateshead – the old Tyne Bridge. Built around 1250, this ever-busy crossing must have been a striking sight to travellers coming from north or south.

The bridge was lined with shops and houses at the section nearest the Gateshead side and there was a chapel dedicated to St Thomas the Martyr (Thomas a Becket) at the Newcastle end.

Two gateway towers were built on the bridge, one close to the Gateshead end and the other between the third and fourth arches on the Newcastle side. The Newcastle tower was used for a number of years as a

The Magazine Gate, built in the 17th Century at the Newcastle entrance to the Old Tyne Bridge.

prison. It is also known that a hermitage or chapel was situated on the crossing and this may well have been in part of the tower.

Another gateway tower, the Bridge End Gate, is believed to have stood at the end of the bridge on the Newcastle side. If it existed, it was demolished to make way for a new entrance building, the Magazine Gate, which was built in the 17th Century.

In 1339, the bridge was badly damaged by a flood and 120 people were drowned. Despite this disaster, the crossing survived and was repaired.

Roger Thornton, a rich merchant and mayor of Newcastle during the late Middle Ages, is said to have

St Thomas's Chapel at the Newcastle end of the Old Tyne Bridge

Left, a detail of the Thornton Memorial Brass in St Nicholas Cathedral, Newcastle, depicting Newcastle mayor Roger Thornton and wife Alice, right the 17th Century Newcastle Guildhall

left six marks a year in his will for a priest in the hermitage to say prayers for his soul.

Thornton, who came from Hartburn parish in Northumberland, was said to have arrived in Newcastle as a virtually penniless young man and to have become "the richest merchant that ever was dwelling in Newcastle". An old saying about him recalls his rags-to-riches story: "At the West Gate came Thornton in with a hap and halfpenny and a lambskin."

The wealthy merchant gave endowments to churches of the town and funded the building of the Maison de Dieu (House of God), an almshouse founded in 1412 on the eastern side of the old Town Chamber and Court, later replaced by the Guildhall, on the Quayside.

The almshouse was dedicated to St Catherine. Sometimes referred to as Thornton's Hospital, it housed nine poor men and four poor women. Part of the building was used by the Merchant Adventurers' Company.

Thornton's impressive memorial brass, which depicts Roger and his wife, Alice, as well as their numerous children, can be found in the city's St Nicholas

An engraving by John Hilbert of the Tyne Bridge in 1727, looking up the river. The arches appear much higher than they actually were.

Cathedral. The benevolent Newcastle merchant and mayor died in 1429.

The old Tyne Bridge was the scene of great pageantry in 1503 when Princess Margaret, daughter of Henry VII, arrived in Newcastle. She was on her way to marry James IV of Scotland. Accompanied by a sumptuously dressed train of nobles, the princess was met on the bridge by the mayor and aldermen on foot.

Prominent among Margaret's retinue was the mounted Earl of Northumberland, dressed in colours of gold, crimson and purple. He was followed by footmen in the same colours and riders in gold jackets. The mayor then mounted his horse and led the royal procession into Newcastle.

Children on one of the gateway towers on the Newcastle side of the bridge sang hymns and played musical instruments to welcome the royal guest. Princess Margaret stayed the night at the house of the Austin Friars in the town.

However, her marriage to the King of Scotland was to last only 10 years. James IV lost his life fighting the English at the Battle of Flodden in 1513.

Two views show ruins of the Old Tyne Bridge after the disastrous flood of 1771.
The lower painting is by Wilson Hepple. © Laing Art Gallery, Newcastle upon Tyne (Tyne & Wear Archives and Museums)/Bridgeman Images

A curious story told about the old Tyne Bridge concerns a ring owned by a Mr Anderson, a member of a leading Newcastle merchant family. Around 1559, Anderson, who was also an alderman of the town, is said to have been fingering his ring as he talked to a friend while they stood on the bridge. He may have been leaning over the parapet as they conversed. The ring then accidentally dropped into the Tyne.

Not long afterwards one of Mr Anderson's servants bought a fish – possibly a salmon – in a Newcastle market and the ring was found inside the fish. As 18th Century town historian John Brand puts it, the ring "was most unexpectedly restored to its owner". The story undoubtedly has a ring of truth.

The end for the old Tyne Bridge came in 1771 when a major flood swept large sections of it away, including most of the shops and houses. Six people were drowned and two were reported to have died afterwards of 'fright'.

Nine houses fell into the Tyne and one of them was found floating, more or less intact, eight miles down river at Jarrow Slake. It is recorded that a dog and cat were found still alive on the ruined building. They were among the survivors, but after 500 years the old bridge had vanished into history.

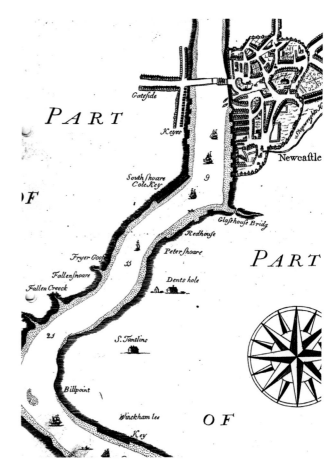

A map marking the position of the Old Tyne Bridge, the only bridge between Newcastle and Gateshead for over 500 years.

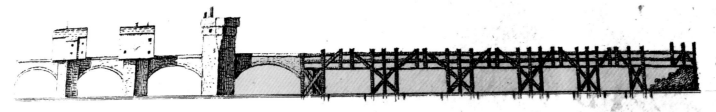

The former Keelmen's Hospital on City Road.

The Keelmen's Hospital

For hundreds of years the River Tyne was a troublesome waterway to sail along because of its sand banks, shallows, tortuous bends and islands. Ships often found it difficult to navigate its waters up to Newcastle and were unable to sail further upstream than the town's quayside.

The arches of the old Tyne Bridge and its 18th century replacement were too low to allow larger sailing vessels to pass up river, where many of the early coal pits were situated, and the water at this point was too shallow.

At low tide, ships that had reached Newcastle were frequently grounded on the sand of its quayside. It was sometimes possible to wade across the river at the point where the High Level Bridge was later built.

Yet despite this difficulty, the Tyne became of major importance to the North East and Britain as the result of vast reserves of coal found in County Durham and Northumberland. From the 13th and 14th centuries onwards the coal was mined and exported from the region in ever increasing quantities. Expansion was particularly marked in the second half of the 16th century.

That expansion of output continued into the 20th Century. Shipments of coal and coke from the Tyne reached their peak in 1923, when more than 21 million imperial tons left the river. An earlier peak of over 20 million had been achieved in 1911.

By the 16th and 17th centuries, small craft had appeared that were able to navigate the tricky

A loaded Tyne keel.

The Keelmen's Hospital c1890.

waterway loaded with the precious, dusty cargo and bring the coal down river to the collier sailing ships waiting in Shields Harbour at the mouth of the Tyne or in the lower reaches of the river below Newcastle bridge.

These small boats were known as keels – small distinctive vessels that were manned by equally distinctive crews, most of whom lived next to the river in the Sandgate district of Newcastle.

When 'off duty' and at leisure the keelmen were said to have had a taste for colourful, stylish clothes. They are recorded as wearing short blue jackets, yellow waistcoats and bell-bottom style light grey trousers.

During their heyday in the 17th and 18th centuries,

keels were the most numerous craft passing Newcastle Quayside. They numbered hundreds. Keels are mentioned in records as early as the 14th century.

The keel was an oval-shaped, very broad-beamed boat with a flat bottom. It was generally about 40ft long and its open-topped, oblong hold took up most of the space in the centre of the boat. When needed, it was propelled by two oars, the longest of which – known as a swape – was also used as a rudder.

When conditions were favourable keels employed sail power using a single mast. However, the main motive force was provided by the tides. Long poles known as 'pouys' were used to move the craft away from the side of the shore or in other conditions in shallow water.

The crew generally consisted of a skipper, two men - known as 'keel bullies' - and a boy, who was known as a 'pee dee'. After taking on their cargo at riverside loading quays or jetties known as staiths, the keelmen would use the ebb tide to drop down to the ships waiting in Shields Harbour or to vessels moored in the river below Newcastle bridge.

On reaching their destination, they would unload the coal by casting it up into the waiting ships using shovels. As can be imagined, casting up was a difficult task requiring great strength and endurance.

The keelmen would then wait for the incoming tide to carry them back up river, often using sail power to assist their passage. The round trip might take 12 to 15 hours.

The Keelmen's Hospital on City Road in Newcastle stands as a testament to the charity of these hardy workers. Between 1697 and 1699, they formed a charity to build the hospital, which opened in 1701 as a residential home for elderly, sick or infirm keelmen and their wives or widows.

Featuring a handsome clock tower and a central, open quadrangle, the hospital cost £2,000 and the keelmen paid for it themselves. Money for the fund was deducted from their wages for each working journey they made.

These sturdy workers are remembered in the celebrated Newcastle song, The Keel Row, but perhaps their greatest memorial is the hospital they founded on the banks of the Tyne.

A drawing showing keels sailing through the Georgian Tyne Bridge.

A section of the Town Walls in the 18th Century.

Three views of gates in the Town Walls during the 18th Century.

The Siege of Newcastle

In 1644, during the Civil War, a Scottish Covenanter army of around 30,000, commanded by Alexander Leslie, Earl of Leven, besieged and bombarded Newcastle. The royalist mayor, Sir John Marley, led the 1,700 defenders. They held out for 10 weeks against these great odds.

The approach of the Scots had been expected and William Cavendish, Marquis of Newcastle, at this time governor of the town, drafted in extra soldiers to strengthen the garrison. He ordered some of the suburbs outside the northern and south eastern walls to be set on fire to prevent the enemy using them as cover. Sandgate was one of the districts chosen.

The Scottish general moved onwards with the majority of his army, leaving several regiments to keep an eye on the town. He captured Sunderland and South Shields and later took his forces south to take part in the Battle of Marston Moor, near York.

Marston Moor was a resounding victory for Parliament, to which the Scottish army was allied. In August, Leven returned north to begin the main siege of Newcastle.

By this time, the Earl of Callander had arrived on the banks of the Tyne, having crossed the border with 10,000 men to reinforce Leven's army. Callander made his headquarters at Gateshead after dislodging royalist forces from the Windmill Hills area. These royalist men retreated across the bridge into Newcastle. Callander then placed five batteries of cannon on the Gateshead side.

Several of his regiments crossed the Ouseburn using a bridge made from keel boats and set up positions outside the eastern walls of Newcastle.

Leven also used a bridge of keels, this time to cross the Tyne, and set up his headquarters at Elswick on the western side of the walls. He spread his forces along the western and northern outskirts.

The town was now surrounded and subjected to regular cannon bombardment.

John Storey's painting of how Newcastle must have looked during the Civil War. Right, sections of the Town Walls can still be seen around the city.

However, cannon fire did not force the defenders into submission. On several occasions, Leven called upon the mayor, aldermen and burgesses to surrender to avoid further bloodshed, but this was refused.

Many people were killed, but the exact number is unknown. There was also extensive damage to buildings, including All Saints (All Hallows) and St Andrew's churches. Unsurprisingly, there were a considerable number of people in the town who thought surrender would be the wisest course.

The Scots were almost certainly aware of the discontent amongst sections of the population and shot leaflets over the walls in an attempt to persuade the townspeople that they should press the mayor to surrender.

William Lithgow, a well-travelled Scot who was present at the siege, was impressed by the Town Walls. He wrote: "The walls here of Newcastle are a great deal stronger than those of York, and not unlike the walls of Avignon, but especially of Jerusalem; being all three decorated about the battlements with little quadrangled turrets; the advantage resting only with Newcastle in regard to 17 dungeon towers fixed

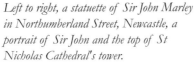
Left to right, a statuette of Sir John Marley in Northumberland Street, Newcastle, a portrait of Sir John and the top of St Nicholas Cathedral's tower.

about the walls (and they also wonderfully strong), which the other two have not...".

In his account of the siege, Lithgow describes in detail the way the walls were heavily fortified by the defenders. For instance, he states that "all the gapes of the battlements were shut up with lime and stone, having a narrow slit in them through which they might murder our soldiers and secure themselves from a just revenge".

Other defensive measures included the construction of an earthwork fort outside the walls at Shieldfield. This fort had been built a short time before the enemy's arrival in February and had defied a Scottish attempt to capture it. In addition, the Castle was strengthened and cannon placed on top of the Keep.

Lithgow describes Newcastle's defenders: "...they were but 800 of the trained band and some 900 besides of volunteers, pressed men, colliers, keelmen and poor tradesmen, with some few experimental officers to overtop them, which were at last overtopped themselves".

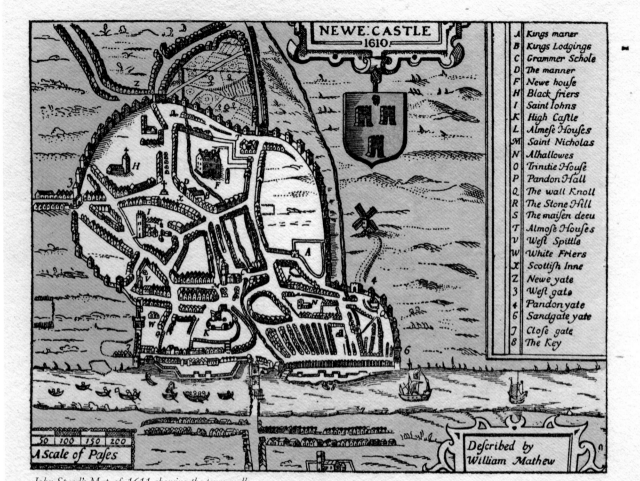

A	Kings maner
B	Kings Lodgings
C	Grammer Schole
D	The manner
F	Newe house
H	Black friers
I	Saint Iohns
K	High Castle
L	Almese Houses
M	Saint Nicholas
N	Alhallowes
O	Trintie House
P	Pandon Hall
Q	The wall Knoll
R	The Stone Hill
S	The maisen deeu
T	Almose Houses
V	West Spittle
W	White Friers
X	Scottish Inne
Z	Newe yate
3	West gate
4	Pandon yate
6	Sandgate yate
7	Close gate
8	The Key

NEWE:CASTLE 1610

Described by William Mathew

A Scale of Pases

John Speed's Map of 1611 showing the town walls.

Early 19th century Newcastle historian Eneas Mackenzie tells us that the garrison used "every effort" to annoy the besiegers. He states: "In frequent sallies from the postern gates they stormed the trenches of the Scots, who were kept perpetually on the alert in order to repel these desperate attacks".

The Scottish forces threatened to demolish the magnificent lantern tower of St Nicholas Church by directing cannon fire towards it. However, the mayor, Sir John Marley, shrewdly placed Scottish prisoners in the tower and the threat was never carried out.

On October 19, 1644, the Scottish launched their final assault. They used prolonged cannon bombardment and mines planted with gunpowder, which had been driven under the walls by Elswick and Benwell pitmen, who may well have been pressed men rather than volunteers.

The breaches were made near several of the important gates and towers – the Whitefriar Tower, West Gate, Close Gate, New Gate, the Carliol Tower, and Sand Gate.

The Scots eventually gained the upper hand, forcing their way into the town. Mackenzie says that at the breach near the Whitefriar Tower defenders on horseback charged the attackers three times, but when reserves arrived the Scots poured into the streets.

On the south eastern side of the walls, Callander and his soldiers climbed through a breach near the Sand Gate and advanced to the Sandhill "with colours flying and roaring drums".

According to Mackenzie "numerous fugitives" from the walls had retreated to the Sandhill, and now, finding themselves surrounded by the enemy, "laid down their arms and called for quarters" (asked for mercy).

Men holding out at the Pilgrim Street Gate put up a strong resistance, being among the last to surrender. Other major flashpoints of the desperate hand-to-hand fighting were at the breach near the Carliol Tower, where many officers and soldiers of the garrison were killed, and close to the New Gate where a garrison captain fought alongside his men "until surrounded by an overwhelming force".

Even after the Scots had captured the town, Sir John Marley and around 300 defenders – including a group of Scottish nobles and gentry – held out in the Castle Keep for a few days longer before surrendering.

There was rejoicing in London at news of the town's capitulation. Parliament had considered it vital that Newcastle be taken to ensure resumption of coal supplies to the capital.

After the siege, some of the townspeople blamed Marley for the loss of life and destruction, that, they pointed out, had resulted from his refusal to surrender earlier. Mackenzie tells us that immediately after surrendering the "gallant mayor was almost torn to pieces by the mob".

Sir John was imprisoned in the Castle for a while and then sent to the Tower of London. However, he managed to escape to the Continent.

To the credit of Leven and his army, it seems there was no slaughter of townspeople after the surrender and no major pillaging, although some thefts from poorer homes were reported. Mackenzie states that the town's hutch (a large strong box) was rifled and a number of documents destroyed.

Following the restoration of the monarchy in 1660, Newcastle began using the motto 'Fortiter Defendit Triumphans – 'Triumphing by a Brave Defence', believed to have been conferred upon the town by Charles I. Although Newcastle had been captured by the Scots, it seems that Charles felt the royalist townspeople had triumphed in spirit. Sir John Marley lived to tell the tale. He was reinstated as mayor.

A King Attempts to Escape

For around nine months in 1646-47, Charles I was held prisoner by the Scots in Newcastle. The hapless monarch was kept under what today would be called 'house arrest' at the Newe House, later known as Anderson Place, a large mansion which occupied a site approximately where the Lloyds Bank building now stands in Grey Street.

The Newe House had been built by the wealthy merchant Robert Anderson in around 1580. It possessed extensive grounds between the Nuns Field and Pilgrim Street. This grand residence was the most prominent feature in the upper part of the town.

During his time in Newcastle the king was closely watched by the Scottish soldiers but was able to leave the mansion and take exercise by walking the streets. It is recorded that Charles was also allowed to play golf on the Shieldfield outside the eastern Town Walls.

In December 1646, a Dutch ship, which had been sent from the Continent to rescue Charles from his captivity, arrived in Shields Harbour. The master of the vessel is said to have journeyed to Newcastle and communicated with the king by clandestine messages. The ship had been sent by Charles' wife, Queen Henrietta Maria.

A night time escape at Christmas was planned. However, when the appointed time arrived the winds proved unfavourable for sailing. The attempt was called off. Later, the king tried to escape a second time but he drew back after seeing how closely the house and grounds were guarded.

The would-be rescue ship then sailed to Hartlepool where the mayor was believed to be a royalist and a third escape attempt was planned. Sir Robert Murray, a close and loyal attendant of the king, sent a message to the Hartlepool mayor about the arrangements. Unfortunately for Charles, the letter was somehow intercepted by the mayor of Newcastle and was given to the Earl of Leven, commander of the Scottish forces occupying the town.

Accompanied by Sir Robert Murray, the king attempted to free himself from the Scots a third time. The two men crept from the mansion and its grounds at night and it may have seemed curious to them that no guards were in sight on this occasion.

Charles and Sir Robert then made their way along the banks of the Lort Burn towards the Tyne, where a boat was believed to be waiting to take them across the river. It had been arranged that horses would be provided on the southern bank for the journey to Hartlepool. From there, the ship would spirit the king to freedom.

However, when they reached the middle section of The Side they saw lanterns amid the darkness. Scottish soldiers had been waiting for them. The attempted escape had been doomed to failure.

From that time onwards, Charles was confined to his rooms at the Newe House and much more closely guarded. The walks in the town and the golfing on the Shieldfield ceased.

Later in the 17th Century, the Newe House was sold to the prominent Newcastle businessman Sir William Blackett. It changed hands again in 1782 when it was bought by George Anderson. His son, Major George Anderson, renamed it Anderson Place. It is not known whether these Andersons were descendants of the merchant Robert Anderson who had founded the house.

Anderson Place was demolished in the 1830s to make way for Richard Grainger's redevelopment of central Newcastle. Today, a plaque on the Market Street side of the Lloyds Bank building records the fact that the tragic king, executed by the Parliamentarians in 1649, once lodged in the mansion – an unwilling guest of the Scots.

King Charles House, now demolished, with the King Charles Tower flats behind. Charles was said to have rested at the house in between sessions of golf on the Shield Field.

Anderson Place, Newcastle, where Charles I was held under house arrest. The King's attempt to escape failed.

An early view of the Newcastle
Infirmary, which opened
in the 18th Century

Breakthrough at the Infirmary

The increased development of industry in the North East during the 18th century, including coal mining, led to an increase in accidents and to a pressing need to treat the victims.

The same century saw the foundation of one of the most important hospitals in Newcastle's long history, a hospital which was a major step forward for the care of the sick and injured. This was the Newcastle Infirmary, situated at the top of Forth Banks, where the Life Science Centre stands today.

The Infirmary lasted for more than 150 years, and from the 1870s onwards witnessed great advances in surgery and medical hygiene. It can be regarded as the first Newcastle 'hospital' in the modern sense of the word.

The Newcastle Infirmary was set up in 1751 and its foundation was made possible by a subscription fund established as a result of a letter to a local newspaper. The anonymous letter, to the Newcastle Courant, was from a mysterious benefactor signing himself or herself as 'B.K.'. His or her identity was never revealed. However, it was rumoured to be a young surgeon named Richard Lambert.

The writer's call for a subscription fund to set up the hospital proved to be a resounding success. Supported by the press, a committee was formed and soon donations were pouring in. Among the most prominent supporters of the scheme was Newcastle Corporation, which made a gift of the land at Forth Banks on which the Infirmary would be built and also contributed £100 towards the fund, a large sum in the 18th century.

The scheme proceeded at great speed. The enthusiasm of its supporters led to the hospital being opened even before the new building was erected. A house was acquired in Gallowgate and it began to receive patients in May 1751. Soon afterwards, there was a need to accommodate more patients and this led to the hiring of rooms in neighbouring houses.

It was not long, however, before building work on the Infirmary at Forth Banks was started. The foundation stone was laid on September 5, 1751, by the Bishop

1st edition Ordnance Survey map from 1864 showing the location of the Infirmary near Newcastle Central Station.

of Durham, the Right Rev Joseph Butler. On October 8, 1753, the hospital was opened to receive its first patients. One of its first surgeons was Richard Lambert, the young man credited with writing the letter that had started the project.

Initially, 90 beds were provided and in the first year 167 in-patients and 178 out-patients were received.

These admissions were by subscriber's letter. This meant that only patients recommended by people who had given money to fund the hospital could receive care and treatment. During this period only the poor used hospitals and there is little doubt that many failed to gain admission. The wealthy were treated in their own homes.

The Newcastle Infirmary c1850.

The hospital admitted many patients injured in accidents, and surgery was a principal part of its work. In 1774, the governors of the institution decided to exclude fever patients from its wards.

Yet there was compassion in evidence. Newcastle historian Eneas Mackenzie, writing in the 1820s, asserts: "Persons meeting with sudden accidents, or labouring under diseases requiring immediate help of surgery, are admitted, without recommendation at any hour of the day or night." All other patients were admitted by a recommendation letter and only on a Thursday.

Despite the recommendations, it seems the conduct of some patients in the early years was not always beyond reproach. Surgeon George Haliburton Hume, in his History of Newcastle Infirmary (1906), declared that "disorderly, dirty and drunken" habits led to strong reprimands from the House Committee. There were occasional complaints from patients about the food and drink. Hume describes an amusing episode in 1754 when a complaint about the meat and beer was judged by the committee to be without foundation. The complaining patients were severely reprimanded and ordered to have toast and water for a week.

It was a distinctly unsympathetic reaction, but the committee seems to have taken on board part of the complaint. They ordered that the quantity of malt in the beer should be increased. At this period a small brewery was situated within the hospital grounds.

A number of 'house visitors' were appointed to the hospital to comfort the patients and perhaps also keep an eye on proceedings. The house visitors in earlier years were expected to attend the funerals of patients, presumably those buried in a cemetery that had been set up in the hospital grounds.

During the second half of the 18th century and early 19th century only a small number of nurses were employed at the Infirmary and their pay was low. Hume suggests that it was likely that much of the time patients were left to nurse each other. Convalescent patients probably shared the nurses' task of looking after the more seriously affected patients.

A significant step forward in the training of nurses came in the late 1860s with the appointment of a nurse superintendent who could provide the

The old infirmary site in 1995

several instances have occurred when two patients have been put into one bed". Two more extensions to the hospital were built during the 19th Century to tackle overcrowding, as demand for hospital treatment grew.

The year 1858 brought a serious crisis. Major outbreaks of sepsis – infection of wounds, often after surgery – struck the Infirmary wards, old and new. These infections – often then referred to as 'hospital disease' - included erysipelas, a serious skin condition.

Another sepsis scourge was pyaemia which, according to Hume, "in former days had so often stepped in to mar the success of many a planned operation". This condition invaded the wards again. Pyaemia proved fatal before the introduction of antibiotics.

necessary education. During the early years of the hospital the few nurses that were employed had been untrained and most were probably unable to read or write.

As well as the scarcity of nursing staff, another drawback beset the institution; throughout much of its life the wards suffered from overcrowding and an excess of patients only added to the risk of infections spreading. Between 1801 and 1803 an extension was built in an attempt to solve the problem. The new wards were divided into small apartments in the belief that his would combat the spread of infection. However, it was soon evident that the additional accommodation provided little relief from the overcrowding.

In 1804, the House Committee told the governors that more beds were "crowded into some of the apartments than they were intended to contain, and

A carbolic spray container, manufactured in Newcastle and almost certainly used at the old Infirmary. Now in the Newcastle University Robinson Library collection.

The last patient leaving the old Infirmary in September, 1906.

The next three years were also badly affected by sepsis and further serious outbreaks continued to occur into the 1860s, reaching a high point in 1867. However, within a decade the situation was to change. In 1874, a new senior house surgeon was appointed, George Beatson, who brought about a vast improvement. He had worked as a house surgeon with Joseph Lister, the pioneer of antiseptic technique, in Edinburgh.

Beatson introduced Lister's methods into the hospital and there was an immediate improvement. Carbolic acid sprays during operations and the use of carbolic acid in the washing of hands and on surgical instruments became the norm. Carbolic acid (sometimes termed 'phenol') was also sprayed on dressings.

A report on the state of the Infirmary in 1875 stated that there had "not been a single case" of sepsis during the year. The antiseptic method had proved to be a major breakthrough in saving lives.

Jesmond Dene and, inset, Lord Armstrong of Cragside.

The Philanthropist

Lord Armstrong of Cragside presided over an industrial arsenal that produced deadly weapons of war, yet in stark contrast he gave to his native city of Newcastle the leafy Jesmond Dene and Armstrong Park and funded other improvements which benefited its people.

William Armstrong was born in 1810 in Shieldfield, on the eastern side of the town centre. He was the son of a prosperous merchant. In 1847, Armstrong and several business partners founded the Elswick Works to the west of Newcastle's town centre, which began by manufacturing his invention, the hydraulic crane, and other hydraulic machinery.

Later, his company branched out into the fields of armaments and shipbuilding. In fact, the Elswick Works became one of the largest arms manufacturing centres in the world and from 1885 began launching numerous warships for many countries.

The Imperial Japanese Navy was one of its most important customers. Between 1893 and 1906 the Japanese took delivery of nine warships from the Elswick Shipyard.

In the 1850s, William Armstrong also developed a light artillery gun, which was more accurate and mobile than the heavy muzzle-loading guns used by the British Army during the Crimean War. Another of his inventions was the hydraulic accumulator, a device that enabled water-powered machinery to be used in situations where sufficient water pressure was not available or impractical.

His success as an inventor and businessman was, however, accompanied by extensive philanthropy. Indeed, the list of his endowments is impressive.

In the 1880s, Armstrong gave Jesmond Dene and Armstrong Park to the people of Newcastle for their enjoyment and recreation and today people can still appreciate these green oases amid the urban environment of Newcastle.

Armstrong College, which was established with financial help from Lord Armstrong and, inset, a group enjoying Jesmond Dene's main waterfall.

In 1859, he contributed towards the fund to build the Northern Counties School for the Deaf by the Great North Road on the edge of the Town Moor.

He also played a leading role in the foundation of the city's Fleming Memorial Hospital for Sick Children, near the school for the deaf. He provided the money for the hospital's new out-patient department in City Road, which opened in 1896.

In 1871, Armstrong donated money towards the establishment of Newcastle's College of Physical Science, which was set up two years later. It became known as Armstrong College in 1874, eventually amalgamating with the School of Medicine to become King's College, Durham University. It was the forerunner to the establishment of Newcastle University.

In the early 1870s he donated money for the building of a new operating theatre at the old Newcastle Infirmary at the top of Forth Banks and in 1885 helped to finance the construction of a new wing to the hospital known as the Ravensworth Wards.

A crowd at the unveiling of the statue of Lord Armstrong outside the Hancock Museum, now the Great North Museum, in 1906.

Lord Armstrong died in 1900 at Cragside, his home in the Northumberland countryside, close to Rothbury. He was aged 90.

A statue of this 19th Century industrial magnate and inventor stands at the junction of Barras Bridge and Claremont Road in the city. It is sited outside the Great North Museum: Hancock, formerly known as the Hancock Museum.

The position of Armstrong's memorial is fitting because of his strong support for the Hancock. Lord Armstrong and his wife, Margaret, donated a total of £11,500 towards the building of the museum, which was completed between 1878 and 1882. This was, of course, an enormous sum in those days. He also gave an important collection of fossils to the institution.

The bronze statue depicts the great inventor, philanthropist and industrial chief standing holding a scroll of drawings and at his feet one of his favourite little dogs, a terrier, possibly a Dandy Dinmont.

On a screen wall below the figure are reliefs showing tugs pulling a vessel through the Swing Bridge, which was designed and largely built by Armstrong's company, and a crane loading a heavy gun on to a warship at the company's Elswick Works. The statue is the work of sculptor William Hamo Thornycroft and was unveiled in 1906.

In the same year, Newcastle's Royal Victoria Infirmary was opened. Lord Armstrong's great nephew and heir to his fortune, William Watson-Armstrong, had given £100,000 towards the building of this fine new hospital, which replaced the old Infirmary. It was around a third of the cost of construction and equipment. The first Lord Armstrong had already donated £3,000 towards the fund.

Money that had been generated by the production of guns and warships was thus, by an extreme irony, used to save lives and relieve suffering.

Yet there were other benefactors, many without great wealth. A total of £20,000 had been contributed towards the hospital by "working men of the district". The opening ceremony was performed by Edward VII on July 11, 1906. The monarch declared that it was "a satisfaction for us to know that the workers have given so generously towards the fund".

FLOODED MINES

The numerous large-scale mining disasters in the North East coalfield claimed the lives of many pitmen and boys. The majority of these tragedies were the result of explosions caused by methane gas, known to the miners as firedamp. In addition, coal dust could greatly increase the power of such blasts.

However, the two worst mining accidents in Newcastle were caused by flooding rather than explosions. The water burst in on unsuspecting miners from old, abandoned workings that had become flooded.

The first of these two disasters occurred at Heaton Main Colliery in 1815 when 75 men and boys died as the result of an inrush of water. Two pitmen encountered the water as they carried out boring to extend a drift tunnel. Worried by the sudden flooding, they told a boy to run and warn the other miners of the danger. He was to advise everyone to head for the shaft and escape.

The lad, who may have been very young, started off on his errand, but the talk of the men about the danger and the gushing of the water had frightened him. He was alone in darkness without company. Instead, he hurried to the shaft and was drawn to bank.

Meanwhile, the inrush of water increased and developed into an unstoppable flood. An engineer, William Miller, tried to warn the men to head for the surface, but he lost his life as he was engulfed by the water which soon filled up the area around the bottom of the shaft, blocking the only way of escape for the miners.

A total of 41 men and 34 boys were now trapped underground in part of the Heaton workings which remained clear of water. Would-be rescuers tried to reach them by using old shafts, but without success.

It was nine months before the bodies of these 75 tragic miners were recovered. They were found to be high above the water level and had been forced to slaughter a pony for food. The water which caused

A sketch of the flooding at Heaton Main Colliery from Louis Simonin's 'Of Mines and Miners', (1868).

the disaster had burst in from disused workings of the older Heaton and Jesmond collieries which had been abandoned in the 18th century.

More than 100 years later there were echoes of the Heaton Main disaster when the View Pit of Montagu Colliery suffered a similar tragedy and 38 miners lost their lives. This pit was situated on the western edge of Scotswood. The accident was the worst disaster to hit the Great Northern Coalfield between the two world wars.

The tragedy happened on March 30, 1925, when the Montagu View Pit was engulfed by an inrush of water from old mine workings. They turned out to be those of the former Paradise Pit, abandoned in 1848.

The water burst through around half an hour after a deputy had fired two shots in the Brockwell Seam, the lowest part of the mine

The shots broke up a section of coal forming part of the 'wall' between the old and new workings. This 'wall' was now too thin to withstand the pressure of water. The deputy and hewers had, of course, been unaware that the old workings were so perilously close.

A trickle was reported by one of the hewers about 15 minutes after the shot-firing. A boy was sent to alert the deputy, Joseph Robson, who returned and decided to ask his young son, also working in the mine, to fetch an overman. Moments later the water burst through with great force. The deputy heard the noise, turned back towards the coalface and saw the flood rushing towards him.

Joseph's son, a putter and two pony drivers escaped, as well as a group of other miners who had waded their way out. The deputy also escaped, but not before he had turned inbye to another area where men were working and led them to safety.

An overman, Sam Evans, was lost when he went inbye in an attempt to rescue others, but was cut off by the rising water. Another man, deputy William Johnson, was also lost as he tried to save his 'marras' (workmates).

Many of the 38 victims at the Montagu View Pit were drowned and others, trapped by the flooding, succumbed to chokedamp. This condition is caused

by a very low level of oxygen in the atmosphere and relatively high level of carbon dioxide.

The accident might have been avoided had the deputies and overmen had access to plans of the old workings, which it was later revealed did exist.

Author A.J. Cronin included scenes based on the Montagu disaster in his novel, The Stars Look Down, published in 1935.

A memorial to the tragic 38 men and boys stands in St John's Cemetery, Elswick, overlooking the Tyne. It features the statues of a miner and the Good Shepherd.

The memorial is a reminder that the pitmen and boys of the Northumberland and Durham coalfield, which included the collieries of Newcastle, made a key contribution to fuelling Britain's industries and providing heating and lighting to millions, but many lost their lives or suffered injury as a result.

Memorial in St John's Cemetery, Elswick, to the men and boys who died in the Montagu View pit disaster of 1925.

Icebreakers for Russia

In 1882, Armstrong's armaments and engineering business at Elswick merged with Charles Mitchell's shipbuilding company which operated a yard at Low Walker in the East End of Newcastle. The resulting company was known as Armstrong Mitchell.

Another change came in 1897 when the Armstrong Mitchell business amalgamated with the Manchester-based firm of Sir Joseph Whitworth to become Armstrong Whitworth.

The Low Walker Yard, which had been founded by Aberdeen-born Charles Mitchell in 1852-53, made a noteworthy contribution to the Tyne's shipbuilding reputation. The yard's output included icebreakers for Russia and the pioneering oil tanker Gluckauf, completed in 1886, the prototype of the modern day tanker. The company went on to produce more than 120 oil tankers.

Low Walker launched mainly merchant vessels, but a number of warships were also constructed. The cruiser Naniwa (sometimes referred to as the Naniwa Kan) was built at the yard for the Japanese Imperial Navy. Following the launch, in March 1885, a dinner was held at the County Hotel, Newcastle, at which Sir William Armstrong presided. In a speech he told guests, who included Prince Yamashino of Japan, that "the ship that had been launched was for the service of a country which was never likely to come into collision with our own peace-loving country".

The Naniwa was completed in early 1886 and was moved down river to Jarrow Slake as preparations began for her delivery voyage. A Japanese crew had arrived on Tyneside to man her. However, just as things seemed to be going well, tragedy struck.

Takezo Fukamachi, who bore the rank of paymaster on the ship, had a serious fall aboard the vessel and died from his injuries. The paymaster is buried in St John's Cemetery, Elswick, his grave marked by an impressive obelisk. The Newcastle Daily Journal described the Japanese officer as "one who, by his kind disposition and gentlemanly bearing, won the respect and goodwill of all those who had the honour of his acquaintance".

Below, the Russian icebreaker Sviatogor, built at Low Walker and, right, the gravestone of Japanese ship's paymaster Takezo Fukamachi in St John's Cemetery, Elswick.

The Low Walker Yard built over 90 vessels of various types for Russia and Charles Mitchell, together with his business partner Henry F. Swan, set up a shipbuilding yard for the Tsarist government in St Petersburg. Several warships were built there under the company's direction.

In recognition of his services, Tsar Alexander II made Charles a Cavalier of the Order of St Stanislaus, a rare honour for a Briton.

In 1895-1898, the Low Walker Yard carried out a very ambitious project – the delivery of an icebreaking train ferry to the shores of Lake Baikal in the middle of Siberia. The ship, appropriately named the Baikal, was designed to carry passengers, carriages and trucks across the lake between two sections of the Trans-Siberian Railway.

The Baikal was constructed on a slipway at Low Walker, taking under a year to complete. She was then dismantled and the different sections and pieces were marked and shipped from the Tyne to St Petersburg. From there, the parts were transported in about 6,900 packages by rail and river to Irkutsk, the largest town near the western side of the lake. The items were then carried by pony-drawn sledges to Lake Baikal.

The first consignment of sections had left Low Walker in 1896 and only in late 1898 did the last consignment reach its destination, a village on the lake shore. The task then began of putting the ship together again.

This work was led by a team of engineers from Tyneside whose journey to Siberia must have been something of an adventure. The Baikal was launched into the lake in June 1899 and after fitting-out entered service the following year. The completion of this project had been a remarkable achievement.

Yevgeny Zamyatin, naval architect and novelist. He lived in Jesmond for over a year while supervising the construction of Tyne-built icebreakers. This portrait is by Boris Kustodiev

The list of Russian icebreakers from Low Walker also included the Yermak (sometimes spelt Ermack), of 1899, the Sviatogor and the Saint Alexander Nevsky, both completed in 1917.

The building of these last two ships was supervised by Russian naval architect Yevgeny Zamyatin, who lived for over a year in Jesmond, Newcastle, and later became a distinguished author, best known for his dystopian novel, We. This book is considered to have been a significant influence on George Orwell's novel, 1984.

The characters in We live in an authoritarian state where life is ordered with mechanical precision and freedom is sacrificed to ostensible happiness. People are known by numbers instead of names.

Zamyatin was also inspired by his stay in Newcastle to write a short novel, entitled Islanders, in which he gently satirised the residents of Jesmond.

This talented Russian drove a Renault motor car and it is likely to have become a familiar sight to the workers at the Low Walker Yard. The Renault may also have been familiar to workers at the nearby Wallsend and Neptune yards, for during his stay in Newcastle the Russian novelist also supervised the construction of several small icebreakers built by Swan Hunter & Wigham Richardson.

By the time of Zamyatin's return to Russia in September 1917, the Tsarist government, which had sent him on his mission to the Tyne had been overthrown.

Charles Mitchell had died in 1895. Using profits from the shipyard, Mitchell had financed the construction and decoration of the magnificent St George's Church at Jesmond, and today its bell tower is still a prominent Newcastle landmark.

The church, near Charles' former home at Jesmond Towers, features beautiful mosaic tiles, fine marble and impressive woodwork carved by renowned Newcastle artist Ralph Hedley. St George's is perhaps Charles Mitchell's greatest legacy to the city.

Zamyatin passed away in 1937. However, one of his Tyne-built icebreakers still survives, the Sviatogor. Now a floating museum, she is moored in St Petersburg and her name has been changed to the Krasin. Looking at the ship today, it is strange to think that her hull first took shape on the banks of the Tyne in Newcastle, far from her Russian homeland.

The Best Little Fellow

Burt Hall in Northumberland Road, Newcastle, is the former headquarters of the pitmen's trade union, the Northumberland Miners' Association. It stands as a lasting memorial to Thomas Burt, leader of the union during the 19th and early 20th centuries.

The Northumberland Miners' Association, originally known as the Northumberland Miners' Mutual Confident Association, was founded in 1863-1864 and Thomas Burt was elected its secretary in 1865 at the age of 27.

Thomas was born in 1837 in a row of cottages near North Shields, the son of a pitman. He and his family moved to Whitley (now Whitley Bay) while he was still a small boy. His father, Peter, worked in a colliery there.

Afterwards the family moved to Seghill Colliery. His father was a Primitive Methodist and an ardent trade unionist. During a major strike of miners in 1844 the family were evicted from their colliery-owned tied cottage at Seghill. The young Thomas witnessed the family's furniture and belongings unceremoniously brought out of their cottage and dumped in the street. Other miners' families were evicted at the same time. The evictions were overseen by constables armed with swords.

The family later moved to County Durham. At the age of 10 Thomas became a trapper boy working ventilation doors at Haswell Colliery, and he later worked as a donkey driver at the same pit. During this period he narrowly escaped being crushed to death by a descending pit cage. A miner saw the danger and pulled the lad to safety with only moments to spare. His hours of work were so long that on another occasion he fell asleep, exhausted, while on trapper duty.

Thomas Burt went on to work as a pitman at several other mines, including Sherburn Colliery in County Durham, and a long stint at Seaton Delaval Colliery, Northumberland. Other pits where he was employed included New Hartley, Choppington and Cramlington.

Burt Hall, right, former headquarters of the Northumberland miners' union, which was opened in 1895

"Tommy Burt is the best little fellow that ever stepped in shoe leather."

Becoming an active trade unionist like his father, in 1865 he took over the reins of the Northumberland Miners' Association. At that time the membership of the union was around 4,000, which included men in the collieries of Newcastle. In 1873, the Northumberland Miners' Picnic, the annual gathering of the county's miners and their families, was held on Newcastle's Town Moor. The event was also held in the city in 1881, 1901, 1902, 1905 and 1908.

At the 1874 general election Burt stood as a radical labour candidate for Morpeth, with Liberal Party support. He won and became one of the first two miners elected to Parliament. The pitmen's leader served as MP for the constituency until 1918, a period of over 40 years.

Burt was one of the first so-called Lib-Lab MPs. These were working or 'labouring' men who sat in the House of Commons with Liberal support. In 1892, Liberal Prime Minister William Gladstone appointed him Parliamentary Secretary to the Board of Trade and he served in this post for three years. The man who had begun his working life in the most underprivileged circumstances as a trapper boy in the darkness of a mine was now a member of the government. It was a remarkable achievement.

A journalist, writing in the 1890s, declared that the union leader was 'plain spoken only when he sees that a straight word of counsel may help his brother, but he is never censorious, and there is always a kindly brotherliness about him'. A friend of Thomas said:

Thomas Burt

Today the Northumberland Miners' Picnic is held at Woodhorn Museum   ©*Richard Kenworthy*

'Tommy Burt is the best little fellow that ever stepped in shoe leather.'

Of his chairmanship of the Trades Union Congress in 1891 an observer wrote: 'It was a magnificent illustration of the sheer force of moral character. It was superb. The adroitness, the tact, the nimble-wittedness, and the good nature and self-possession which characterised him are beyond praise.'

Thomas Burt died at his home in Brandling Village, Newcastle, in 1922 and is buried in a family grave in the city's Jesmond Cemetery. He had retired from his post as secretary of the union in 1913.

The facade of Burt Hall carries an inscription paying tribute to the distinguished trade unionist. The building was opened in 1895 and is now a part of Northumbria University. The inner main entrance door is decorated with stained glass windows depicting two miners' safety lamps and on the upper floor a meeting hall contains a fine stained glass window featuring shields with images of picks, shovels, a lamp, tub and other mining emblems.

The roof of Burt Hall is surmounted by the statue of a miner with a pick over his shoulder. This sculpture is based on one of the figures in the popular Ralph Hedley painting of two pitmen, entitled Going Home. The statue might be described as the crowning glory of the building and can be seen as a memorial to all Northumberland miners

Town Moor Racing

Horse racing on Newcastle's Town Moor began in 1721 and continued there for nearly 150 years. The race meetings had been transferred to Newcastle from Killingworth Moor, where they had been held since the first half of the 17th century.

A cattle disease outbreak led to the cancellation of the races in 1749 and 1750. However, they were restarted in 1751 and from this time onwards the meetings were held from just before Whitsun to the week nearest Midsummer Day, in other words in late June. They now extended over five and sometimes six days.

Race Week on the Town Moor proved to be extremely popular, with thousands of people flocking to watch the horses, drink, gamble, meet friends and enjoy the stalls and sideshows. Pitmen were said to be particularly numerous among those attending.

Among the performers in the shows was the multi-talented Billy Purvis of Newcastle, a famous comedian, musician, singer and conjuror, who for many years toured the North East with his troupe of entertainers.

During the week, more than 120 tents were put up on the field and there was a considerable amount of heavy drinking. Another attraction, before it was outlawed, was cockfighting, a cruel but very popular sport in the early days of the races.

In 1800, the two-storey Grandstand, described as an "elegant stone edifice", was erected close to the finishing post and from its galleries there was said to be a fine view of the whole course.

The Grandstand was situated a short distance to the east of the present-day junction of Grandstand Road and Kenton Road, approximately where the Moor Court flats stand today. The finishing stretch of the course ran along the southern side of this section of Grandstand Road.

The Grandstand was largely destroyed by fire in 1844, but the building was reconstructed and lasted until well after racing ceased on the Moor. It eventually became part of a school for boys, but was demolished in 1909 following closure of the school.

In around 1822 a project was launched to change the route of the racecourse to avoid a particularly difficult slope. The outlines of the old and 'new' courses can still be traced today.

One of the earliest of the Town Moor racing trophies was the Gold Cup, given by Newcastle Corporation. The council was clearly happy to encourage the economic benefits that Race Week brought to the town.

However, the most famous race was the Northumberland Plate – dubbed the Pitmen's Derby because of the large number of miners who attended. It was first run in 1833 and the winner was a colt named Tomboy, ridden by Bob Johnson. However, the greatest success in the event was enjoyed by jockey Tommy Lye, who won the Plate no less than six times during the late 1830s and early 1840s.

During this period the course also witnessed a famous mare, Beeswing, show off her talent. She won the Newcastle Gold Cup six times. Born and trained in Northumberland, Beeswing was victorious in most of her races, and her son, Newminster, was a St Leger winner.

Despite the evident success of the annual meetings, suspicions arose that some races were being fixed and there was concern about the heavy drinking that took place. The year 1881 saw the last of the meetings on the Town Moor and the races were transferred to High Gosforth Park from 1882. This meant that tighter regulation could be enforced to combat any corruption and disorder.

After around 160 years of crowd-packed excitement the racing was gone from the Moor, but the grassland did not fall silent and large crowds still flocked there for a few days each year. The reaction against the heavy drinking at the races led to the establishment

Thomas Bewick's depiction of the Town Moor Races.

The Grandstand overlooking the Town Moor racecourse.

NEWCASTLE GRAND STAND.

of an alternative attraction on the Moor – a Temperance Festival that became known as The Hoppings. This eventually developed into the huge annual funfair that is still held during the last week in June, Race Week.

The Hoppings is said to be the largest non-permanent fair in Europe and occupies most of the eastern section of the Moor alongside the Great North Road. The early Hoppings included foot races, bicycle races, football matches and other sports. Reporting on the first Town Moor Temperance Festival in 1882, the Newcastle Daily Chronicle declared: "On whatever part of the Moor the eye rested, a moving mass of human beings was witnessed. It is doubtful whether the most successful of the Plate Days ever drew together such an immense assemblage, and the opinion was quite freely expressed that never in the annals of the great Northern race meeting had so many people been seen on and around the course."

In front of the Grandstand, and occupying the same part of the Moor as during the race meetings, many tents were set up and stalls erected for the sale of food and non-alcoholic drinks. The organisers were evidently determined that the principles of temperance should be upheld.

The Northumberland Plate races at Newcastle Racecourse in High Gosforth Park and The Hoppings on the Town Moor still flourish today as two of the city's most abiding traditions.

The Town Moor Festival.

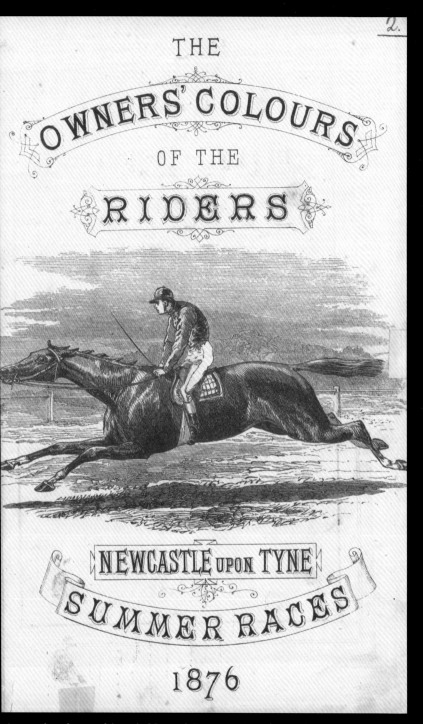

THE
OWNERS' COLOURS
OF THE
RIDERS

NEWCASTLE UPON TYNE

SUMMER RACES

1876

A rare coloured racecard from the Newcastle Races of 1876

THE OW

Mr. Armstrong.	Mr. H. Ashton.	Mr. T. Bates.	Mr. R.
Black, red cap.	No Colours recd	White, blue belt and cap.	Black an hoo
Mr. J. Chapman.	Mr. R. Chilton.	Mr. J. R. Close.	Mr. R. J.
Blue, white cap.	Orange, green sleeves and cap.	Purple, white stripes.	Red, wh blue
Earl Durham.	Mr. Elliott.	Mr. R. Feather-stone.	Mr. R. Fo
Purple, straw sleeves	Purple, white stripes.	Black.	Green, bl and
Mr. W. Hender-son.	Mr. E. Hirst.	Mr. T. Holmes.	Mr. R. H
Geranium red, white belt, black cap.	Blue, white belt, blue cap.	White.	Union jack sleeves
Mr. McCaffrey.	Mr. R. Manfield.	Mr. Masque.	Mr. S. Me
Green and white bars.	No Colours recd	Violet, pink cap.	Green, sca
Mr. Perkins.	Mr. G. Reynold.	Mr. T. Richard-son.	Lord Ros
Turquoise, violet sleeves	Mauve, black sash,	Red, white belt.	Rose, vin

[Printed] in Colours, and Published by ANDREW REID, Prin[ters], [C]urt Buildings, Akenside Hill, Newcastle-upon-Tyne.

Rider	Colours
H. Bragg.	[choco]late, black cap.
Mr. J. T. Best.	Blue, white belt and cap.
Mr. H. Bird.	Violet & white hoops, black cap.
[Mr.] Boulton.	[Scar]let, blue sleeves and cap.
Mr. Bowes.	Black and gold.
Mr. W. Brown.	Black.
Mr. C. Bush.	Red, black and gold belt and red cap.
Mr. R. Carr.	Light blue, straw sleeves and cap.
Capt. Carruther.	Light blue, white cap.
Mr. Cashman.	Lavender, red cap.
[Mr.] J. Coates.	[whi]te, black cap.
Mr. R. Cowan.	Yellow, black cap.
Mr. Cookson.	Purple, straw sleeves.
[Mr.] G. Crook.	[Whi]te, solferino cap.
Mr. J. Cowan.	Yellow, fawn cap.
Mr. C. J. Cunningham.	Green, white hoops.
Mr. M. Dawson.	Black, gold belt & cap.
Mr. T. Dawson.	Dark blue, black cap.
Mr. J. G. Donkin.	Blue, white hoops.
Capt. Dove.	White, red sleeves, black cap.
[Mr.] Gardner.	[..], green sleeves and cap.
Mr. T. Green.	Black, red sleeves and cap.
Mr. T. Gretton.	Orange, purple belt and cap.
Mr. J. Gilby.	[..], straw & white belt and cap.
Mr. J. S. Godson.	Blue, white spots.
Mr. Gomm.	White, orange belt and cap.
Mr. H. Hall.	Maroon, white sleeves.
Capt. Haworth.	Green, black cap.
Mr. W. Harvey.	Green, black cap.
Mr. Heneage.	Yellow, brown sleeves and cap.
[Mr.] Horncastle.	[..], grey sleeves.
Mr. Hunter.	Magenta, orange cap.
Mr. W. S. M. Innes.	Black, crimson belt and cap.
Mr. R. Johnson.	Purple, straw belt.
Mr. J. Johnstone.	Dark blue, silver braid.
Count De Juigne.	Scarlet and orange hoops, black cap.
Mr. E. Lascelles.	Light brown, black cap.
Mr. A. Louis.	White, scarlet hoops.
Mr. P. Lucas.	Yellow, scarlet sleeves and cap.
Mr. T. Lunn.	Orange, blue cap.
[Mr.] Melville.	[..], blue sleeves and cap.
Mr. Messenger.	Blue, gold hoops.
Mr. W. W. Moffat.	Black, yellow cap.
[Mr.] D. Newsome.	[Bl]ack, gold stars.
Mr. W. Nicholls.	White, red spots, red sleeves and cap.
Mr. Northern.	Pink, black hoops.
Mr. G. Oliver.	Green, white belt, black cap.
Mr. J. Osborne.	Chocolate, black cap.
Mr. R. Osborne.	Chocolate, blue sleeves and cap.
Mr. R. Peck.	Blue, orange sleeves.
[Mr.] Robertson.	[choco]late, yellow
Mr. W. Robinson.	Scarlet, blue cap.
Mr. W. Sadler.	Scarlet, blue sleeves
Mr. T. Sayer.	[Sc]arlet, blue belt
Mr. J. Snarry.	
Mr. Sanderson.	
Mr. J. Shepherd.	
Mr. E. Stephenson.	
Mr. J. Smith,	
Mr. R. Stobbs.	

Above, the scene of the Town Moor explosion today. Below, a newspaper sketch of the scene of the Town Moor explosion which resulted in the death of John Mawson (right) in 1867.

The John Mawson Tragedy

Joseph Wilson Swan was the joint developer of one of the most revolutionary inventions of all time – the electric incandescent light bulb.

Born in Sunderland in 1828, he initially trained in pharmacy on Wearside but in 1848 became a partner in the Newcastle manufacturing chemist and pharmacy business of John Mawson.

It took many years of experimentation for Swan to develop his incandescent light bulb into practical working form. This revolutionary lamp used a carbonised incandescent filament.

Eventually, in December 1878, he gave a demonstration of his lamp to members of Newcastle Chemical Society and in February the following year to a gathering of the Newcastle Literary and Philosophical Society on the city's Westgate Road.

Also in 1879, Swan's incandescent filament lamp was used to illuminate Mosley Street, Newcastle, making it the first street in the world to be lit by this epoch-making invention. Mawson's shop and chemist works were in Mosley Street and they too were lit by the bulb. These experimental moves proved the efficacy of the invention.

A further development came in 1880 when Swan's incandescent lamps were installed at Cragside in Northumberland, the home of Sir William Armstrong. At Cragside the lamps were powered by hydro-electricity.

In 1881, Swan, Sir William Armstrong, John Theodore Merz and Robert Spence Watson set up a factory in South Benwell, Newcastle, to manufacture the bulb. It was the first such works in Europe. In December the same year, the Savoy Theatre in London, home of the Gilbert and Sullivan comic operas, became the first public building in the world to be lit entirely by Swan's incandescent lamps.

In the USA Thomas Edison had developed a very similar bulb, even though both men had been working independently of one another. Although initially involved in a legal dispute over the invention, Swan and Edison eventually came to an agreement and together formed a new company. The resulting business was known as 'Ediswan'.

Unfortunately for Newcastle, the South Benwell factory closed in 1887 and production of the lamps was moved to Ponders End in the South of England.

Swan, who was knighted in 1904, improved on his invention by developing cellulose filaments instead of carbonised ones. Many of his experiments were carried out at his home, Underhill, Gateshead, which is generally regarded as the first private home to be lit by his incandescent bulbs.

John Mawson, the Newcastle chemist, had encouraged Swan in his early experiments, which included the development of improvements in photographic processing. Without that encouragement, the inventor might never have achieved such success in the field of electric lighting.

Mawson was married to Joseph Swan's sister and so the two men had family as well as business ties. However, Mawson was to meet a tragic end as the result of an explosion on the Town Moor.

The accident occurred in December 1867, following the discovery of nitro-glycerine which was being stored in the cellar of the White Swan Yard in Newcastle's Cloth Market.

Police officers found eight tins of the explosive and duly informed the magistrates and the Town Clerk. It

Advertisements for Mawson & Swan's business.

was decided to destroy the substance by taking it to the Town Moor and emptying it into the earth at a spot where there was an area of subsidence in the ground caused by the workings of the Spital Tongues Colliery.

Mawson, who was Sheriff of Newcastle at the time, and Thomas Bryson, the Town Surveyor, decided to accompany the material to the Town Moor to see that it was disposed of safely. A number of other people also walked with the cart carrying the nitro-glycerine.

SWAN'S
FACTORY.

Joseph Swan and, top, his blue plaque in Newcastle.

He decided to have these three remaining cannisters buried in a different spot on the Moor – on a hill area a relatively short distance away.

Mawson instructed Sub-Inspector Wallace to cover the place into which they had poured the liquid with soil, while he, Bryson and the others set off for the hill with the three cannisters.

Sub-Inspector Wallace had just completed his task and was about to join the others when he heard a violent explosion. Wallace felt the earth shake and saw pieces of clothing and other articles flying high up in the air. When he reached the west side of the hill where the blast had occurred, he found PC Bain, Thomas Appleby, and the labourer, James Shotton, dead. They had been dreadfully injured by the blast.

A boy, Samuel Bell Wadley, was lying seriously injured in a hole in the ground. The body of an unidentified man was also found. Lying badly injured on the eastern side of the hill was Town Surveyor Thomas Bryson. On top of the bank was Mawson. He too was severely wounded.

The three were taken to the Newcastle Infirmary at Forth Banks. The boy passed away about two hours after reaching the hospital. Mawson and Bryson died the following night.

An inquest jury returned the verdict: "That death has been caused by an explosion of nitro-glycerine accidentally, and the jury are unanimously of the opinion that the law in reference to the storing of nitro-glycerine has been grossly violated in this case."

When they arrived, Bryson, the cartman and a labourer, Sub-Inspector Wallace of the town's police, and PC Donald Bain drew the corks from the eight cannisters. They then emptied the liquid into the depression in the earth.

After this was done three of the cannisters still felt as if they contained something weighty. Mawson ordered the men to take off the ends of the containers and it was found that some of the nitro-glycerine had crystallised and was sticking to the tins.

STEPHENSON

The Geordie Lamp

The statue of a man stands at the junction of Westgate Road and Neville Street in Newcastle city centre. Many people hurry by with scarcely a glance at this monument to George Stephenson, the pioneering locomotive engineer who played a leading role in ushering in the era of steam railways.

Nearby, is the city's elegantly impressive Central Station and only a short distance further away is the magnificent two-deck High Level Bridge across the River Tyne. This bridge was designed by Stephenson's son, Robert, and completed in 1849. The huge iron structure, supported by sandstone pillars, was built to bring the railway from London into Newcastle for the first time.

A short distance beyond the Victorian grandeur of the Central Station, on the banks high above the river, lies the site of Newcastle's Forth Street locomotive works, where the famous engines Locomotion No. 1 and Rocket were built. Although known as the Forth Street Works, it was actually situated in South Street, a turning off Forth Street.

George Stephenson came from a poor, underprivileged background, yet through his spirited efforts, his passion for the steam locomotive and mechanical genius, he became one of the world's most famed engineers.

Stephenson did not invent the locomotive, but he played a major role in perfecting it and making it into a workable iron horse of incalculable benefit to the world. He also demonstrated conclusively that steam railways were an efficient form of transport and pioneered the early techniques of steam railway construction.

George was born in 1781 in a cottage on the banks of the Tyne at Wylam, only a few miles west of Newcastle. He was one of six children. The family's poverty meant that his parents and five of the children, including George, all had to live together in one room of the house. The remaining rooms were occupied by three other families.

His father, Robert, like countless other men in the North-East, found employment in coal mining. He was a fireman, stoking the pumping engine at Wylam Colliery.

At the age of 14, George began following in his father's footsteps and became assistant fireman at Dewley Burn Pit, not far from Newcastle. Then, following the closure of this mine, he became a fully fledged fireman, working at two other pits in the area. Afterwards he joined his father at Water Row Pit, Newburn, on the western side of Newcastle.

It was at Water Row that his mechanical talents came to the fore. George began to gain a reputation for his ability to mend machinery. He was so successful that at the age of 17 he was put in control of the Water Row pumping engine.

In 1801, he obtained a job as a brakesman at the Dolly Pit of Black Callerton Colliery. This meant he was in control of the winding engine that brought coal to the surface and lowered and raised men in and out of the mine.

Soon, George's life was to take a new turn when he fell in love with a woman 12 years his senior. She was Frances Henderson, known as Fanny, who worked as a servant at a farm in the Black Callerton area where George had lodgings.

George and Fanny were married at Newburn Church in 1802. The newly-weds moved to Willington Quay near Wallsend, on the banks of the Tyne east of Newcastle. They lived in one room.

Sailing ships, returning from their coal voyages to London, would unload ballast at various points along the Tyne. Hills of ballast would be formed as more and more material was added.

One of these hills was at Willington Quay and George's job was as brakesman in charge of the stationary engine which pulled waggons full of ballast to the top of this mound by means of cables.

George and Fanny's only son, Robert, was born in the cottage at Willington Quay in 1803. The following year the family moved to Killingworth Colliery, a few miles to the north of Newcastle. The young father had been appointed a brakesman at the colliery and the family lived in a house at West Moor, later to be known as Dial Cottage.

It was in this home that the couple's daughter, named after her mother, was born in 1805. However, the baby only lived for three weeks. Worse was to come. Tragedy struck again when Fanny, who had been in poor health, died of consumption at the age of 37 the following year.

In 1812, Stephenson's talents as a man who was good at fixing machinery were recognised when he was appointed enginewright by the Killingworth Colliery owners, the Grand Allies. The 'allies' were four powerful businessmen headed by Thomas Liddell, who later became Lord Ravensworth.

It was in 1814 that Stephenson constructed his first steam locomotive at the Killingworth Colliery workshops. It was a step which would lead him to fame and fortune.

However, less well-known nationally is Stephenson's invention of a safety lamp for miners. Mining has always been a dangerous occupation, but in the early

19th century it was many times more hazardous than it later became.

One of the greatest perils facing the men and boys as they worked underground was methane gas, known to the miners as firedamp. This gas, sometimes referred to in Stephenson's day as hydrogen, had the potential to cause fatal explosions if it came into contact with the naked flame of a candle or oil lamp.

Common in many pit workings, methane made the possibility of an explosion an everyday risk for the miners, who might die of burns, crush injuries or carbon monoxide poisoning in the wake of the blast (afterdamp). Another peril which sometimes developed following an explosion was chokedamp, also known as blackdamp, which produced a suffocating atmosphere because of very low oxygen levels and high carbon dioxide levels. In addition, a gas explosion in combination with coal dust could create a wall of flame that would sweep through the workings.

Killingworth Colliery, along with other mines in the North-East, suffered its share of such tragedies, the danger being posed by methane fissures in the rock. For example, more than 20 men were killed as the result of gas explosions at the colliery in 1806 and 1809. Stephenson had personal experience of these tragedies and it is not surprising that he should have brought his mind to bear on the problem.

It was in August 1815 that Stephenson began carrying out experiments to devise a safety lamp protected from the methane, then often referred to simply as hydrogen. Some of these experiments took place down one of the Killingworth Colliery pits and involved carrying lighted candles near 'blowers'. These were sites where methane issued strongly from fissures. Such tests were, of course, extremely dangerous.

Stephenson's eventual idea was to surround an oil flame with a protective glass cylinder and to encase this in a tin cylinder. Three versions of the lamp were produced, each one an improvement on the other. In the first version, air was allowed to reach the flame by means of a tube at the base of the lamp. In the third version, air was admitted to the tin cylinder and to the top and base of the glass cylinder by numerous small holes.

Meanwhile, the nationally famous scientist Sir Humphry Davy was also working on the problem and he too drew up plans for a safety lamp, which were similar in principle, although not in form, to Stephenson's.

Davy had visited Tyneside during his investigations and there is evidence that he had access to information about Stephenson's lamp. However, Stephenson pipped Davy to the post by having his lamp in use first.

Davy announced his plan for a lamp at a meeting of the Royal Society in London in November 1815. The following month, Stephenson demonstrated his lamp, which became known appropriately as the Geordie Lamp after its inventor, at a meeting of Newcastle's Literary and Philosophical Society. However, unlike

Davy's, the Stephenson lamp was already in use at Killingworth Colliery. He had taken it into the mine in October 1815 after having it made by a Newcastle tinsmith. The glass tube was supplied by the Northumberland Glass House.

Two years later Stephenson stated: "This lamp was tried out in Killingworth Colliery on 21st October, 1815. The idea I had long entertained and the drawing was shown to several persons employed in that concern, two months before the day above mentioned, when I carried it with safety into a part of the mine where a strong blower of hydrogen was coming off. An experiment which was immediately repeated in the presence of two persons employed in that concern."

One of the men who accompanied Stephenson on that momentous occasion was his friend, Nicholas Wood, who became head viewer (manager) of the colliery.

By the time Stephenson gave his lecture to the Newcastle Literary and Philosophical Society, the third, improved version of his safety lamp had been used in the mine.

Despite this success, a furious dispute erupted when Sir Humphry Davy was acclaimed nationally as the inventor of the safety lamp and awarded £2,000. It was even alleged that Stephenson had in some way borrowed Davy's ideas. Stephenson's supporters in the North-East were stung by these claims, asserting that their man had been the inventor.

An interior at the Stephenson Works before restoration.

North-East men of wealth and power, including the Grand Allies, Charles Brandling and William Losh, strongly defended Stephenson. In 1817, a North-East committee of inquiry was set up, which met at the Assembly Rooms in Newcastle, to look into the issue. Witnesses testified to the committee that Stephenson's lamp was the first in use, and his name was cleared of the allegation that he had borrowed Davy's ideas.

The committee "ascertained that as early as August 1815" Stephenson "was busied with various experiments upon the air proceeding from blowers in coal mines". The enginewright was accordingly awarded £1,000 and a silver tankard by his supporters. During his visit to Tyneside, Davy had seen a safety lamp devised by Sunderland physician Dr William Clanny. Clanny had initially invented a form of lamp

George Stephenson's Cottage in West Moor.

that proved to be impractical, but he went on to develop a much better one. In the 20th century many of the safety lamps in use were based closely on Clanny's improved design. His lamp featured a large window for the light. Miners in the Northumberland coalfield called their lamps 'glennies' and this term is believed to be derived from Clanny's name. The Clanny design had proved to be the most influential in the long-term.

During the 19th century, the Geordie Lamp was routinely used at Killingworth Colliery and probably at a number of other North-East mines. Yet the Davy lamp seems to have been the most widely adopted lamp in the region at this period.

However, the Davy version, which was surrounded by a wire gauze, did not have a glass cylinder like the Geordie. Occasionally, a draught might cause the flame from a Davy to pass through the gauze and make contact with explosive gas. The Geordie, with its protective glass cylinder, did not suffer from this defect, the glass enclosing the flame.

In addition, the upper part of the Davy was said to have a tendency to become overheated, another hazard in gaseous conditions. The Geordie's glass cylinder was again an asset because it helped to prevent this happening. However, in around 1820 Stephenson re-designed his lamp, surrounding it with a gauze, similar to Davy's, although he retained the vital glass cylinder.

Both the Geordie and Davy safety lamps undoubtedly saved countless men from death, but they were far from perfect and they emboldened mine owners to send men into gaseous seams that had hitherto been thought too dangerous. These lamps provided only a dim light and miners were still sometimes tempted to use candles. The risk of explosions was far from being eliminated.

What was really needed was greatly increased ventilation to expel gas from the mines. This only came later in the 19th century with the introduction of powerful mechanical fans, operated by steam, and later by electricity.

Despite this, the safety lamp, of whatever type, proved to be a superb gas detector that could warn men of the presence of methane. The behaviour of the flame was the key to determining the level of gas. This proved to be its greatest asset.

A sketch of the Great Fire of Newcastle in 1854.

Cholera and Fire

In 1853, Newcastle was hit by a major outbreak of cholera. This serious disease even affected patients in the town's Infirmary and six died.

The hospital's staff won admiration for the way they dealt with the crisis. As the cholera epidemic raged, the Infirmary opened its doors to all, free of charge, and gave comfort to worried and anxious people. Some presented themselves at the hospital believing they were suffering from early symptoms of the disease and were offered medicine and advice.

The wards of an uncompleted extension to the hospital were used to relieve pressure of numbers during the outbreak, which caused 1,533 deaths in the town. How cholera was transmitted was a mystery to physicians until a doctor who had trained in Newcastle came up with a convincing theory.

The city's School of Medicine originated in 1832 when a small group of physicians and surgeons began giving lectures to medical apprentices in an auction room above the entrance to Bell's Court, a lane off Pilgrim Street.

The initial number of students attracted by the course was eight or nine and they included John Snow, who was to help pioneer the use of chloroform as an anaesthetic. Dr Snow administered chloroform to Queen Victoria when she gave birth to Prince Leopold in 1853 and at the birth of Princess Beatrice in 1857.

Significantly, Dr Snow was the first to advance the theory, which proved to be correct, that cholera was a water-borne disease, caused by pollution from cesspools, drains and sewage and he wrote about ways of preventing this serious illness. Snow accordingly placed great emphasis on the provision of clean water, free from pollution.

Dr John Snow

In 1854, Snow traced the source of a cholera outbreak in Soho, London, to polluted water from a pump in Broad Street, helping to establish the truth of his theory. He persuaded the authorities to have the handle of the pump removed.

His attention had almost certainly been drawn to the question of cholera during an outbreak of the disease while he worked as an apprentice to a Tyneside surgeon in 1832. There were 306 deaths from the illness in Newcastle during this particular epidemic.

The 1853 outbreak of the disease was followed, in 1854, by the Great Fire of Newcastle and Gateshead. This was almost certainly the worst catastrophe in the history of the two towns.

The fire broke out at around 1am on October 6 in a wool factory close to the riverside in Gateshead. The blaze then spread to a neighbouring warehouse where chemicals were stored. This contained sulphur, nitrate of soda, iron, lead, manganese, guano, alum, arsenic, copperas and salt.

The sulphur melted in the heat of the fire and began pouring from the warehouse in purple-coloured liquid form like the lava streams of a volcano. Other substances, such as molten lead, may have added to these streams. The flames also reached a flour mill which was reduced to a ruin.

The spectacle attracted a large crowd, some of them on the Newcastle Quayside and others on the High Level Bridge and the 18th century Bridge that had replaced the medieval Tyne Bridge. A huge number of people also gathered on the Gateshead side. Few if any could have guessed the danger they were in.

Two small blasts were heard and afterwards, at around 3.10am, an immense explosion threw flaming debris across the river on to the Newcastle Quayside area and beyond. The debris included blazing sulphur and wood.

The blast was said to have been heard up to 20 miles away from Tyneside and the fire was seen as far away as North Yorkshire. Gas lamps were blown out, plunging parts of the town into darkness. Windows were shattered, roofs collapsed and stones from buildings were hurled great distances into central Newcastle.

Newcastle's Quayside after the devastating fire of 1854

A total of 53 people died as the result of the catastrophe and a large number were injured. It is recorded that as well as onlookers and residents, the death toll included firemen who had been called to tackle the blaze. They had been concentrating their efforts on the Gateshead warehouse. Hundreds of families, most from the poorer areas near the riversides, were made homeless and a national appeal was launched to help them. This raised nearly £11,000.

Newcastle Infirmary treated 123 injured victims of the disaster and 60 of these were admitted as in-patients. The wards of the new extension to the hospital, designed by renowned architect John Dobson, played an important role in enabling the hospital to cope with this very serious emergency. A new, large accident room, which had opened only two days before the fire and explosion, greatly assisted initial assessment and treatment. Others who suffered injuries were treated at the Gateshead Dispensary.

Properties in many of the chares (narrow lanes or alleys) running between Newcastle Quayside and Butcher Bank (later named Akenside Hill) were engulfed in flames and destroyed. These chares, which dated to medieval times, were gone forever. Among the dead was John Dobson's son, Alexander. He was 26.

Some of the stones from the explosion can still be seen at this memorial near St Mary's on the Gateshead side of the river.

大清㊤女故廬江縣顧世忠之墓 光緒七年歲次辛巳四月二十八日立 宣統三年歲次辛亥閏六月吉日重修

大清故勇山東袞州府榮城縣袁培福之墓 光緒七年歲次辛巳四月二十六日立 宣統三年歲次辛亥閏六月吉日重修

大清故勇福建福州府閩縣連金源之墓 光緒十三年歲次丁亥四月十四日立 宣統三年歲次辛亥閏六月吉日重修

中國北洋水師墓地修繕紀念碑
This plaque commemorates the restoration
of the memorials to five Sailors
of the Imperial Chinese Navy.

中国文物保护基金会尊捐修缮
Funded by
The China Foundation for Cultural Heritage Conservation
2018.12

The graves of Chinese sailors in St John's Cemetery, Elswick, and, below, the Chinese cruiser Ching Yuan.

Chinese Sailors

Armstrong's Elswick Shipyard built vessels for many countries, but the Chinese cruisers Chih Yuan and Ching Yuan attracted much more than the usual level of interest among the people of Newcastle.

The Chih Yuan was the first of the pair to be launched into the Tyne. The ceremony on September 19, 1886, had, to Western observers, several unusual features. No women were allowed to attend and no brass band played as the ship slid down the ways. Instead, cannons were fired from the river bank in salute.

Lord Sudeley, one of the dignitaries attending the launch, spoke about the ship's name when he addressed the reception following the launch. According to him Chih Yuan meant "Go to far places and demolish all you come across." His interpretation produced a gale of laughter from some of the Western guests present.

However, diplomat Mr Fung Lee, who replied on behalf of the Chinese Minister in London, remarked that "there were perhaps not many people who understood Chinese". He went on to give his own translation of the cruiser's name: "There is no distance to which this cruiser cannot extend and no enemies she is not able to overcome." This statement was greeted with applause.

In June 1887, the Chinese transport ship Too Nan entered the Tyne and berthed alongside the grain warehouse on Newcastle Quayside. Aboard her was Admiral W.M. Lang and nearly 600 officers and men of the Chinese Imperial Navy. They had come to collect the two cruisers being built at Elswick and other warships nearing completion at Stettin in Prussia.

Newcastle had played host to seamen of many nationalities, but this sudden influx of Chinese sailors engendered more than the usual level of curiosity. Contemporary accounts describe the dress of the sailors: dark blue uniforms, light blue waist scarves and black turbans. The officers wore close fitting Chinese hats, and dark blue suits with black velvet facings and trimmings.

Members of a rank or grade described as 'secretaries' were resplendent in silken robes of light blue and

The Chinese cruiser Chih Yuan, built at the Elswick Shipyard.

white. Every move of the sailors seems to have been followed with great interest by the people of the city.

When Admiral Lang, accompanied by almost his entire force, attended a performance of a play at the Tyne Theatre and Opera House in Westgate Road it seemed they attracted more interest than the play.

Nearly half of the pit had been reserved for the men. The officers were seated in the dress circle, while Admiral Lang and Captains Kew Pow Chin and Tan Shi Chang occupied a private box.

All 580 of them arrived after the performance had started. They marched up from the Quayside in columns of four. As each officer entered the theatre he presented his card. More than 80 crimson-coloured cards bearing Chinese characters with English translations were handed to the door keepers.

An account in the Newcastle Daily Journal described the scene inside the theatre: "While the drop scene was down they were the cynosure of all European eyes. To English people, the sight of men-of-war men using fans seems very inappropriate but several of the officers, either unaware of the effect they were making or indifferent to it, made use of their fans with all the ease, if not the grace, of a society lady."

The burial of two Chinese sailors in St John's

Cemetery, Elswick, caused the Newcastle Daily Journal to comment: "...the idle curiosity which in Newcastle follows all the walks abroad of the wanderers from the Flowery Land was not allowed to lapse even in the instance where death intervened".

The sailors were, aged 21 and 30. They died in the Newcastle Infirmary at Forth Banks. At 4:00am on June 6, 1887, a contingent of 40 of their shipmates, under the command of Captain Yeh, arrived at the Infirmary. Carefully they wrapped the bodies in white sheets, then placed them in the coffins. Before the lids were secured the dead men's clothes were neatly folded up and laid beside them.

The Chinese coffins were very heavy. They were black, built of strong wood, lined with lead and thickly coated with varnish. It took much effort to carry these coffins from the mortuary on to the waiting hearses. The proceedings were watched by another sick Chinese man from one of the windows of the Infirmary.

The cortege made its way up Westmorland Road. The hearses and the silent column of sailors then climbed Rye Hill and turned into Elswick Road. When the cemetery gates were reached an unexpected reception awaited them. About 200 people had got out of their beds at that early hour to witness the interment. They crowded closely around, determined not to miss a

The Tyne Theatre and Opera House in Westgate Road where the Chinese sailors enjoyed a play.

single aspect of the ceremony.

The graves had been dug close to those occupied by two Chinese sailors who had died of consumption aboard the transport ship Hai Shin while she lay at Elswick Works in May 1881.

After the coffins had been lowered into the graves the contingent of sailors, with their officers to the fore, knelt down in front of each grave in turn and silently bowed their heads to the earth five or six times. They then covered the coffins with soil and finished the funeral ceremony by igniting a heap of joss paper over each mound.

The nurses at the Infirmary paid their respects by sending a pair of wreaths, and two young sisters, the Misses Tailford, laid bouquets of flowers on the graves.

Six days later, again at 4:00am, another sailor was laid to rest near his old comrades. A large crowd again gathered and a police guard was on duty at the graveside. It was reported that on board the Too Nan nine other seamen were suffering from what seemed to be a similar illness.

The gravestones of the three sailors still survive in St John's Cemetery. Two Chinese headstones nearby are those of the men from the transport ship Hai Shin. An inscription fronting the headstones of the three men buried in 1887 included the words: "The

The Elswick cruiser Yoshino, whose guns helped to sink the Chih Yuan.

tombstones of these three and the two neighbouring graves were erected by the officers and crew of the Chinese cruisers Chih Yuan and Ching Yuan."

The Too Nan left the Tyne on June 20, 1887, with 291 of the sailors on board. They were on their way to Stettin to take delivery of two other cruisers. In August, it was the turn of the Chih Yuan and the Ching Yuan to depart the river. They steamed southwards to Spithead to rendezvous with the Stettin ships and a torpedo boat which had been built at Poplar in London.

Within a few days all the newly-built ships had assembled in Spithead. It was not long before they sailed for China via Suez.

The Chih Yuan and the Ching Yuan served the Imperial Chinese Navy for less than 10 years. Both were lost during the Sino-Japanese War of 1894-1895.

The Ching Yuan was sunk by shells fired from a fort at the Battle of Wei-Hai-Wei in February 1895. The Chih Yuan met her end at the Battle of the Yalu in September 1894, during a clash with a Japanese force which included the Elswick-built cruiser Yoshino.

The Chih Yuan tried to ram the Yoshino but failed to hit her faster opponent. The Chinese cruiser was then sunk by gunfire. It was ironic that the fortunes of war had pitted one Elswick-built ship against another.

The Elswick Works, Newcastle

A Illustrated London News sketch showing the arrival of foreign workmen during the engineers' strike.

Battling Engineers

In 1871, William Armstrong's Elswick Works in the West End of Newcastle was gripped by a national strike when engineering workers battled to obtain a nine-hour day. After a five-month struggle against the employers, who strongly opposed the demand, they were successful.

The nine-hour day was first conceded in Sunderland, but the workers in Newcastle and Gateshead came up against a determined resistance by the employers who had retaliated to the strike by bringing in foreign workers. However, the engineers persuaded many of these men to return home.

The striking members of the Amalgamated Society of Engineers, as well as some non-union workers, received financial aid from the Northumberland miners' union. The men were led by John Burnett, who later became general secretary of the Amalgamated Engineers.

Delegates from Britain were sent to the Continent to warn workers in Belgium, Holland, Denmark and Germany against helping the employers by emigration to Tyneside and other areas of the North.

Critics who supported the engineers in their struggle drew attention to the large profits being made by engineering company employers in the North of England.

Although the employers gave way to the nine-hours demand in 1871, a second dispute, from July 1897 to January 1898, ended in defeat for the trade unionists. This struggle was over a demand for an eight-hour day and again involved the Amalgamated Engineers.

On Tyneside, the industrial battle began with a lockout of workers that had been imposed nationally by the Engineering Employers' Federation, an organisation that appears to have been determined to crush the trade unionists.

The masters had taken their action in response to a strike in London for the eight-hour day. On July 13, 1897, all men employed on day shifts in Tyneside workshops owned by members of the employers' federation ceased work. The masters had given notices to 25 per cent of the men and the remaining 75 per cent retaliated by sending in their notices to finish at the same time. It was a clear expression of solidarity.

The Newcastle Daily Journal reported the following day: "Contrary to public expectations there was no demonstration when the men left work at 5 o'clock. At Elswick, at Hawthorn Leslie and at Stephenson's the men came out without any sign of being finished for an indefinite period."

Lord Armstrong's company was a leading member of the employers' federation and the newspaper was critical of the stance he had taken during the nine-hour day dispute in 1871. Armstrong had then stated that a reduction from 59 to 54 hours per week would mean a loss to the employers of 17 per cent and pointed out that his company had to suffer severe competition from foreign manufacturers and those at home.

The Newcastle Daily Journal asserted that Lord Armstrong's forecasts had been "entirely falsified". Evidence for this was that the previous year his firm had made a clear profit of over £368,000.

On July 31, 1897, men demonstrated in favour of the eight-hour hour day at Newcastle's Haymarket. On August 21 a second demonstration was held, this time attended by at least 7,000 people. The workers assembled in Rye Hill and marched, complete with band and banner, to the Haymarket.

They were addressed by several speakers, including Keir Hardie, the pioneer of independent labour representation in Parliament who became the first leader of the Labour Party. Hardie told the crowd that since the employers had on their own initiation forced the eight-hour issue to the fore, the men would take them at their word and say: "You have locked us out because you thought we wanted an eight-hours' day and now we shan't go in till we get it."

He said he looked beyond the dispute to the time when the men would again be called upon, not to decide a lockout or a strike, but to decide whether the men who had locked them out should be allowed to continue to have a monopoly in the government of the country, or whether they as working men, with brains and votes, would also demand to have their representatives in the House of Commons.

Mr T. Wilkinson, secretary of Newcastle, Gateshead and District Trades and Labour Council, put forward a motion: "That this meeting condemns the action of the federated employers in locking out the workmen in the engineering trade, thus causing untold misery and suffering to thousands of innocent men, women and children, as well as unlimited damage to the commerce and industry of this country." The motion was carried unanimously. Wilkinson urged every man present to join a trade union.

However, cracks began to appear in the united front

A sketch of men at the Elwick Works. Engineers at the works won a nine-hour day.

of the engineers. On September 24, a group of men returned to work at Elswick. Several incidents of violent intimidation by strikers did occur during this phase of the dispute and there were a number of resulting prosecutions.

This national struggle was a great strain on the strike fund of the Amalgamated Engineers and by the end of October 1897, strike pay had to be reduced. The position of the engineers continued to deteriorate. On January 18, 1898, they were forced to withdraw their eight-hour day demand. The six-month battle was over.

A ballot was organised by the union to vote on a return to work, but Mr J.W. Thwaites, secretary of Newcastle and Gateshead district branch of the union, was of the opinion that it did not matter much about the result of the vote because the financial position of the Amalgamated Engineers was so poor it was imperative for the men to return to work.

By early February it was reported that 600 men had resumed work at Elswick and others were expected to return soon afterwards.

In 1871, the battling engineers had tasted the sweetness of victory. Now, in 1898, they experienced the bitterness of defeat.

The
North-East Coast
EXHIBITION
Newcastle-upon-Tyne.

Great Exhibitions

An area on the southern section of the Town Moor was known as the Bull Park. It had been the land on which the town's bulls were kept for stud. The area did not open as a park until 1881.

A scheme – first proposed by the North East Institute of Mining and Mechanical Engineers – was drawn up to hold a major industrial exhibition on this land to celebrate Queen Victoria's Golden Jubilee in 1887.

However, the Bull Park was found to be too small for this purpose and Newcastle Corporation and the Freemen of Newcastle agreed to provide extra land from an adjacent area of the Town Moor. This enlarged the exhibition area to around 31 acres, including the Bull Park.

The resulting 1887 Royal Mining, Engineering and Industrial Exhibition proved to be a great success.

Officially opened by the Duke of Cambridge, Commander-in-Chief of the Army, more than two million people attended the event.

It featured a large, rectangular building arranged around a central open-air square planted with flower beds and surrounded by a verandah. A bandstand with a fine roof, which has survived to this day, was erected in the centre of the square. The whole building was lighted by electricity, an innovative feature in the 1880s.

"Splendid selections" of steam locomotives of the period were exhibited by the North Eastern Railway Company, and by locomotive builders Robert Stephenson and Co. and Hawthorn, Leslie & Co. Products of the North East's marine engineering, mechanical engineering and hydraulic industries were also on display, including those of the steel firm

NEWCASTLE-UPON-TYNE
ROYAL MINING, ENGINEERING AND INDUSTRIAL EXHIBITION.
(JUBILEE YEAR, 1887.)
PLAN OF THE NORTH GARDENS.

Top, The buildings that hosted the 1887 Royal Mining, Engineering and Industrial Exhibition and, left, an exhibition programme containing a plan of the North Gardens.

Spencer & Sons, of Newburn, and marine engineering business the Wallsend Slipway and Engineering Company.

The Newcastle engineering, armaments and shipbuilding company of Armstrong Mitchell exhibited a full-size model of a 110-ton gun.

However, perhaps the most impressive feature of the event was a full-size working model of a coal mine, complete with pit ponies, tubs and rail lines. There was also a display of miners' safety lamps. An additional attraction was a model lead mine.

Another important attraction was a replica of the old Tyne Bridge, which spanned a lake based on an old reservoir that supplied water to the town. Much of this lake survives today. The height and length of the model bridge were two thirds of the original bridge's actual size, but the width was the same as the original.

The area where the exhibition was held eventually became known as Exhibition Park, although the names Bull Park or Recreation Ground continued to be used for many years afterwards.

The 1887 event was not to be the only great show held there. In 1929, there was a particularly pressing need for the North East to show off its capabilities. The economy of the region, with its famed heavy industries, was in decline. The Depression had begun to bite hard.

The 1929 North East Coast Exhibition was organised with the aim of promoting the region's trade and boosting its industries and employment. It was opened by the Prince of Wales, later Edward VIII. The opening day was attended by around 75,000 people.

Understandably, the site chosen for the event was Exhibition Park. The buildings were on a grand scale and in the art deco style. Twelve Egyptian-style pylons (tower-like pillars) greeted the visitors at the main entrance in Claremont Road. The North-East's impressive industrial and commercial achievements were shown off in two 'palaces'.

An avenue leading through the site from the main entrance led via boating lake to a third structure, the Palace of the Arts. The lake had been widened and deepened and was created from an old reservoir that had been used to supply water to the city.

Surmounted by a dome, the Palace of the Arts is today the only surviving building from the exhibition. The Palace featured galleries in which paintings, sculpture, photographs and other works, on loan from various North East art galleries and wealthy collectors, were on show.

Flanking the western side of the avenue, the imposing Palace of Industries and Palace of Engineering displayed the skills and products of the region's companies.

In the Palace of Industries, which at 167,000 square feet was the largest of the exhibition's buildings, the many firms represented included the Newcastle and Gateshead Gas Company, the city's two electricity

Photographs taken by Philipson & Son, official photographers for the 1929 North East Coast Exhibition. Courtesy of Ward Philipson Photo Memories.

BOARD AND MAIN AVENUE, NORTH EAST COAST EXHIBITION 1929, NEWCASTLE-UPON-TYNE.

AND PALACE OF ARTS, NORTH EAST COAST EXHIBITION, 1929, NEWCASTLE-

MAIN ENTRANCE, NORTH EAST COAST EXHIBITION, NEWCASTLE-UPON-TYNE.

Philipson & Son photos taken at the North East Coast Exhibition, including souvenir stands and a Carricks restaurant

firms, Newcastle Breweries, which had produced Exhibition Ale especially for the occasion, Andrew's Liver Salts, Smith's Crisps and retailers Bainbridge, Fenwick and Binns.

In the Palace of Engineering, Tyneside companies exhibiting included Vickers-Armstrongs, Swan Hunter & Wigham Richardson, Clarke Chapman, Parsons and Reyrolle. Shipbuilders displayed a wonderful collection of model vessels from North East yards.

There was a stadium for games, sports and parades, an Empire Marketing Board Pavilion, a Festival Hall for concerts, an amusement park with attractions such as a large water chute and a 'Himalayan Railway'

roller-coaster ride. Most unusual of all, a replica 'African Village' was constructed within the grounds. It featured visiting people from West and North Africa.

Visitors also included King Alfonso of Spain, the Sultan of Zanzibar and High Commissioners from countries of the Empire, as well as over four million other people. Gold watches were given to each one millionth visitor.

On the final day, October 26, 1929, just two days before the Wall Street Crash, there was an attendance of nearly 120,000. The North East Coast Exhibition had indeed been an extraordinary show.

More official photographs from the 1929
North East Coast Exhibtion and,
below, the Palace of Arts building which
is now home to Wylam Brewery

The statue of Earl Grey, with decorations for the Great Exhibition of the North, 2018.

Earl of Newcastle

The statue of Charles, 2nd Earl Grey, is the impressive centrepiece of Newcastle and undoubtedly the city's most prominent monument. Grey is famed as the Prime Minister who successfully steered the Great Reform Bill through Parliament in 1832.

The Earl, who was MP for Northumberland, stands on top of his 134ft-high fluted column surveying Newcastle as he has done since 1838 when the statue was erected. The sculpture, by Edward Hodges Baily, is a landmark throughout the city centre. Baily was the sculptor who also created the figure of Nelson in London's Trafalgar Square.

Newcastle's Earl Grey is larger than life at 13ft high, and he stands on a pedestal above a balcony, which is reached by climbing 164 steps inside the column. The column was designed by architect Benjamin Green, of the Newcastle firm of John and Benjamin Green,

who were designers of the nearby Theatre Royal.

Grey is depicted standing in dignified pose and dressed in court attire. He carries a scroll in one hand, presumably the Great Reform Bill itself. The monument is Grade One listed.

In 1941, during the Second World War, Baily's statue was struck by lightning and Grey's head fell to the street below. It was early morning and, very luckily, no one was killed or injured.

A replica head was carved by Roger Hedley, a son of Ralph Hedley, the well-known Newcastle artist. It was eventually installed in early 1948. So for over six years the unfortunate Earl was without his head.

Grey was a leading figure in the Whig party and he believed that electoral reform was necessary to stave

A view from the top of Grey's Monument.

off social unrest or even revolution in Britain. However, he was not a supporter of complete manhood suffrage, and almost certainly not votes for women. Yet the Great Reform Bill was a move in the right direction. It was the first important step on the long road to votes for all – but that journey was not complete until well into the 20th century when women won the vote.

The effect of Earl Grey's 1832 Reform Bill was to enfranchise the upper middle classes. Seats were redistributed to give representation to the growing towns which had expanded as the result of the Industrial Revolution. Gateshead, for example, was given a Member of Parliament for the first time. It was a milestone – but only one milestone. By the standards of today this legislation was a very limited

reform stipulating property qualifications for the right to vote. However, it increased the size of the electorate by around 50 per cent.

Grey made it clear that he regarded the mass of the population as unsuitable to be granted the vote for many years to come. His approach was essentially cautious and conservative.

Earl Grey also led the move in Parliament to abolish slavery in the British Empire and he was a supporter of the movement for Catholic Emancipation. In addition, he spoke against restrictions on civil liberties imposed as a reaction to the French Revolution.

This Northumbrian aristocrat retired from politics in 1834. In retirement, he lived at his home, Howick

Above, the Monument today and, below, Howick Hall.

Hall, close to the Northumberland coast. Grey died in 1845.

The Earl is also famous for his tea. The story is told that when Grey was Prime Minister he was sent a present of blended tea from China. The Earl liked the tea very much – it was flavoured with oil from the bergamot orange. Lady Grey served the tea to her guests in London and it proved a great success. It remains one of the most popular blended teas.

Standing above the Monument Metro Station in the centre of the city and gazing down Grey Street towards the River Tyne from his lofty eminence, this aristocrat should perhaps be given an additional title - "Earl of Newcastle."